In Need of Care

A Play

David E. Rowley

A Samuel French Acting Edition

SAMUEL
FRENCH
FOUNDED 1830

SAMUELFRENCH-LONDON.CO.UK
SAMUELFRENCH.COM

Copyright © 1969 by Samuel French Ltd
All Rights Reserved

IN NEED OF CARE is fully protected under the copyright laws of the British Commonwealth, including Canada, the United States of America, and all other countries of the Copyright Union. All rights, including professional and amateur stage productions, recitation, lecturing, public reading, motion picture, radio broadcasting, television and the rights of translation into foreign languages are strictly reserved.

ISBN 978-0-573-02322-4

www.samuelfrench-london.co.uk

www.samuelfrench.com

FOR AMATEUR PRODUCTION ENQUIRIES

UNITED KINGDOM AND WORLD EXCLUDING NORTH AMERICA

plays@SamuelFrench-London.co.uk

020 7255 4302/01

Each title is subject to availability from Samuel French, depending upon country of performance.

CAUTION: Professional and amateur producers are hereby warned that IN NEED OF CARE is subject to a licensing fee. Publication of this play does not imply availability for performance. Both amateurs and professionals considering a production are strongly advised to apply to the appropriate agent before starting rehearsals, advertising, or booking a theatre. A licensing fee must be paid whether the title is presented for charity or gain and whether or not admission is charged.

The professional rights in this play are controlled by Samuel French Ltd, 52 Fitzroy Street, London, W1T 5JR.

No one shall make any changes in this title for the purpose of production. No part of this book may be reproduced, stored in a retrieval system, or transmitted in any form, by any means, now known or yet to be invented, including mechanical, electronic, photocopying, recording, videotaping, or otherwise, without the prior written permission of the publisher. No one shall upload this title, or part of this title, to any social media websites.

The right of David E. Rowley to be identified as author of this work has been asserted by him in accordance with Section 77 of the Copyright, Designs and Patents Act 1988

Cast in order of appearance:

Shirley
 a girl of thirteen or fourteen
Rita
 the same age
Nobby
 a boy of thirteen or fourteen
Jeff
 the same age

The action of the play passes in the interior of a semi-derelict farm outbuilding on a Saturday morning in spring

Time - the present

To Denise, Lesley, Brendan and Clifford

IN NEED OF CARE

A semi-derelict farm outbuilding on Jeff's farm. A Saturday morning in spring.

On one side is a large double door, one half of which is bolted shut, the other hanging half askew on a single broken hinge. In the back wall is a window about six feet from the ground. It consists of a number of small panes, some of which are cracked or broken, and all of which are covered in grime. Numerous farm implements hang from the walls, horse harness, old hose pipe, shelves with paint pots, etc. There is an old rusty bicycle with only one wheel, and scattered about the floor are small bits of machinery and junk, upturned boxes, straw bales, a large pile of straw partly covered by a tarpaulin, loose straw and a tea chest in which is a motor-cycle carburettor. A strong light is coming through the window and filtering through the partly open door.

When the CURTAIN *rises, Shirley and Rita are concealed under the pile of straw and tarpaulin. Shirley is tough, determined, crafty and distrustful, though underneath her hard shell is a soft centre. She probably comes from a home where her father or brother are convicted criminals, where moral values (as judged by conventional society) are of little account, and where the police and authority are fair game in a jungle society. Rita is extremely sensitive, with a great capacity for love, groping hopelessly for an anchor in life. She is not very bright, weak-willed and easily led by stronger personalities such as Shirley.*

Everything in the barn is quiet and still. Dogs are barking in the distance. Suddenly Shirley's arm comes into view, dropping in her sleep. She stirs, pulls the straw away from her head, rubs her eyes, sits up and scratches herself. She looks at her surroundings with distaste, gets up on to her feet, stiff with cold, rubs her arms and hugs herself against the cold. She is dressed in a school uniform, blouse, skirt and pullover. She moves stiffly to the door and cautiously looks out, right and left, blinking at the brighter light from outside. Then she turns back to the pile of straw.

Shirley Wake up, kid.

There is some movement in the straw. It is Rita, lying on her stomach. She stirs herself slightly and pulls a piece of sacking to herself against the cold. Shirley is now seated on a bale of straw, rummaging about in a large, cheap-looking handbag. She pulls out a crisp pack which contains two or three crisps. She eats these and shakes the remaining crumbs into her mouth. She screws up the empty crisp pack and throws it on to the floor. She rummages again in the handbag, finds nothing of interest, puts it down, and climbs up on the pile of straw to the window, giving Rita a sharp kick as she goes

Rita Ow! (*She moves up into a sitting position, resting on her elbows*)

Shirley goes to the window, rubbing a space in the grime with her elbow to see through

(*Sitting up*) I'm cold.
Shirley Get up, then.
Rita Did you sleep much?
Shirley No.
Rita Nor me. Too cold.
Shirley We'll be all right tonight. You'll see.
Rita (*getting up onto her feet*) I hope so. I don't fancy this lot again. How far is it?
Shirley Where?
Rita To your auntie's.
Shirley Dunno. Not far.
Rita How far?
Shirley (*irritably*) I don't know. About ten miles.
Rita Can we walk ten miles?
Shirley 'Course we can.

Rita picks up the handbag and searches in it

Rita Let's get going right away.
Shirley What for?

In Need of Care

Rita I'm hungry.
Shirley Don't be daft.
Rita Well, I am.
Shirley Walking won't help, it will make you hungrier.
Rita I can't find my money.
Shirley Well, I never took it.
Rita I never said you did.
Shirley You'd better not.
Rita Oh, I remember.

Rita goes over to the straw where she was sleeping and searches. Shirley comes down from the window and goes to the door and looks out

Shirley Some mothers do have 'em.

Rita finds her handkerchief in the straw. It is tied in knots with her money inside

Rita Where are you going, Shirl?
Shirley I'm bursting.
Rita Oh.

Shirley goes out through the door. Rita sits on a bale of straw, unknots her handkerchief and counts her money

Rita Shilling, one and three, one and fourpence, one and five, one and six, one and seven. What can we get for one and seven, Shirl? (*She wraps the money up again, sees and picks up the empty crisp pack*) You've eaten all the crisps. (*She throws the pack down, picks up the handbag, puts her handkerchief and money into it, pulls out a small mirror and lipstick, and starts to apply it rather badly*) Shirl.

Shirley returns

Shirley Stop shouting, you silly cow. Do you want everyone to hear?
Rita Sorry.

Shirley comes over to Rita and rudely snatches the lipstick and mirror

I've got one-and-seven. We could get a cup of tea and some crisps.
Shirley Where?
Rita There must be a caff or something near.
Shirley In this one-eyed hole? Even if there is one, they'd suspect us.
Rita Why?
Shirley In a little place like this.
Rita What are we going to do? I'm ever so hungry. (*She takes out a comb and combs her hair*)
Shirley We'll walk into Frampton. It's only about two miles.
Rita There's bound to be a caff there.
Shirley We're not going to no caff.
Rita But I'm hungry.
Shirley Honestly, Reet, you've got nothing above your neck. We'll spend the money in a supermarket.
Rita What for?
Shirley Well, you can't go into a supermarket and spend nothing, can you?
Rita No.
Shirley So, use your loaf. We go in there and spend the one and seven, and while we are in there we nick enough to keep ourselves going all day.
Rita Oh, Shirl.
Shirley It's as easy as pie.
Rita I don't want to get into no more trouble.
Shirley You're in trouble already, scarpering from school, so a little more won't make much difference. 'Sides, we won't get caught. It's dead easy.
Rita Do you reckon so?
Shirley 'Course it is. They can't prove nothing.
Rita I don't know.
Shirley Oh, for God's sake, Reet. You aren't half chicken. We won't get caught I tell you.
Rita I'm sorry, Shirl. I wish I was as clever as you.
Shirley Well, you're not.

Rita gets up and moves over to the window, looking out

Rita Can't we get going?

Shirley Can you see anyone?
Rita No.

Shirley comes over to look

Shirley Look.
Rita What?
Shirley Over there. Those boys.
Rita They're miles away.
Shirley We'd better wait a bit. Keep watching and tell me what they do. (*She comes away from the window and pokes about in the straw with her foot. She finds a dead mouse and utters an exclamation of disgust*)
Rita What's up?
Shirley There's a rat.
Rita (*joining her*) Let's have a look. Where?
Shirley Just down there by your foot.

Rita sees it and bends down to look at it

Rita That's not a rat. That's a mouse.
Shirley Same thing.
Rita Of course it's not. A mouse is much smaller.
Shirley Well, it gives me the creeps. Us sleeping there with that horrible thing. Don't touch it, Reet.
Rita It's dead.
Shirley Leave it alone.
Rita (*picking it up*) Oh, look, it's lovely. Poor little mouse. Look, Shirl, it's ever so pretty. Look at its sweet little face.
Shirley (*backing away in alarm*) Don't you come near me with that thing. It's horrible.
Rita It's not horrible. It's beautiful. (*She cradles the mouse in her hand and strokes its fur. Then she moves over to and sits on the upturned box*) Poor little mouse, why did you have to die? Why did you die, little mouse? I wish I had found you when you were alive. I would have looked after you and you wouldn't have died.
Shirley Don't be so daft. Throw it away.
Rita I always wanted a mouse. Cathie wouldn't let me have one. I wanted a mouse so much. Poor little thing. Why is God so cruel to make you die? (*She is emotionally moved, and bites her lip to keep back the tears*)

Shirley Reet.
Rita I can't help it. I love it. I'm going to bury it properly.
Shirley You're so soft. Throw it away.
Rita No.

Rita moves towards the door, but Shirley moves quicker and bars her way

Shirley You can't go out there. Those boys.
Rita I'll keep it and bury it later.
Shirley (*looking out through the door*) Rita, the boys. They're coming this way.
Rita Oh God, Shirl, what are we going to do? (*She moves to the window*)
Shirley Ssh! They may not come in.
Rita (*looking out*) Oh God!
Shirley Shut up.

For a few seconds the girls peer anxiously out of the window and door. Suddenly Shirley moves quickly

Quick. Under the straw.

They hurriedly try to bury themselves, using the sacks and tarpaulin
Throw that rat away.
Rita It's not a rat.
Shirley Throw the bloody thing away.
Rita No, no.

They scuffle. Shirley gets the mouse and throws it across the barn

I hate you.
Shirley Shut up

They settle under the straw and keep quite quiet and still, apart from an occasional sniff by Rita

Sssh!

Nobby comes in through the door, followed by Jeff. Nobby is a strong character with a zest for life, but thoughtless and insensitive to the feelings of others. Jeff is a quietly spoken boy, with strong family ties. They are dressed suitably for boys messing

In Need of Care

about on a farm on a Saturday morning. Jeff carries a stick and a large jack-knife

Nobby It will go a hundred miles an hour.
Jeff Who are you kidding? (*He sits down on the upturned box and starts whittling his stick*)
Nobby Bet you. We went eighty-five when I was on the back, and the throttle wasn't nearly wide open. (*He goes and looks at the rusty bicycle, turning the wheel*)
Jeff Will he let you ride it when you're old enough?
Nobby I'm not bothered. I'll get one of my own. Second-hand bikes don't cost that much.
Jeff When I go to work, I'm going to get a car.
Nobby Motor-bikes are better.
Jeff I could take Mum out shopping and things.
Nobby Who wants to take their mum out. A motor-bike is smashing for taking birds out on. (*He finds the old motor-cycle carburettor in the box*) Here, Jeff, look at this. I bet this came off an old bike. (*He brings it to Jeff and shows him*)
Jeff Oh, that. There's some more bits over there.
Nobby Where?
Jeff Just down there by the door.

Nobby moves to the door to look. He stops suddenly and freezes. He has seen Rita's leg sticking out from the straw

Nobby Jeff.
Jeff What?
Nobby Jeff, come here.
Jeff What for?
Nobby Jeff, there's something. Oh, blimey.
Jeff What's up?
Nobby There's a leg.
Jeff A leg?
Nobby A human leg. Sticking out of the straw.

Jeff comes over to look

Jeff Christ. It's a dead body.

Nobby and Jeff stare in horror at the leg, then at each other.

They panic and run out of the barn. After a second or two Shirley cautiously peers out

Shirley They've gone.

Rita's head appears

Rita Now what are we going to do?
Shirley You stupid great nit. Leaving your leg sticking out.
Rita I couldn't help it. I didn't know.
Shirley We gotta get out of here quick. They'll fetch the law.
Rita Ssh!

The girls freeze, listening for sounds

Shirley Quick, pretend we're dead.

The girls pull the straw over themselves and lie very still

Nobby and Jeff enter. They come cautiously to the body, grim-faced, and stare at each other, undecided

Nobby Have you ever seen a dead body?
Jeff No.
Nobby What should we do?
Jeff I think we ought to fetch my dad.
Nobby Do you think we ought to look?
Jeff It might be all smashed up and bloody.
Nobby The leg looks all right. It looks like a girl.
Jeff She might be naked.
Nobby Yes, she might.

Jeff moves towards the door, but Nobby hesitates

Nobby Let's have a look.
Jeff All right, but don't touch it.

Jeff watches as Nobby moves to the head of the "body". Nobby starts gingerly to move some of the straw. He looks up at Jeff.

Jeff Go on.

Suddenly Shirley's hand sweeps up and catches Nobby across the face. Nobby goes sprawling and Jeff jumps in alarm. Shirley sits up. Jeff sees the funny side and roars with laughter

Shirley Sorry to disappoint you, mate.

Rita sits up

Jeff Blimey, there's two of them.
Shirley He can count.

Shirley and Rita stand up, brushing away the straw

Rita We were just having a kip.
Nobby What did you want to go and clout me for?
Shirley So as you didn't get no ideas, like feeling me to make sure if I was really dead.
Nobby Who are you?
Shirley Curious, aren't you?
Jeff You don't live round here.
Shirley So?
Jeff You're trespassing. This is my dad's barn. It's private.
Rita We didn't know. Come on, Shirl, let's go.
Shirley Wait a minute. (*To Jeff*) What's your name?
Jeff Jeff. Why?
Shirley (*to Nobby*) And you?
Nobby Nobby.
Shirley Stiles?
Nobby Yes, as a matter of fact.
Shirley We've got a right one here, Reet.
Jeff His name is Stiles. We just call him Nobby.
Shirley I'm Shirley. This is my mate Rita.
Nobby Hi
Rita Hi. (*Edging towards the door*) Come on, Shirl.
Shirley Shut up. (*To the boys*) No, we don't live here, but we're staying at Rita's auntie's in the village. We went for a walk and felt tired, so we came in here for a rest.
Rita And fell asleep.
Shirley Yes, that's right.

The boys exchange glances

Nobby Who's your auntie?

Rita looks blank, and then turns appealingly to Shirley

Rita Mrs er—er . . .
Shirley Mrs Brown.
Nobby Never heard of her.

Shirley Do you know everyone, then?
Nobby Nearly everyone.
Shirley So if you don't mind we'll be getting along. Sorry to have trespassed. So long. (*She moves towards the door*)
Nobby Wait a minute.
Rita What for?
Nobby I want to speak to my friend.
Shirley Nobody's stopping you.

Nobby takes Jeff's arm and leads him away to one side

Nobby They're lying.
Jeff Yes?
Nobby I'm sure.
Jeff How?
Nobby In the paper this morning.
Jeff Eh?
Nobby In the *Mirror*. Their pictures were. I recognize them.
Shirley Don't you know it's rude to whisper?
Jeff I never saw the paper.
Shirley Hey, you.
Nobby What?
Shirley I'm talking to you.
Nobby Well, belt up.
Shirley Charming.

Nobby goes over to the girls

Nobby I know who you are. You absconded.
Shirley Absconded?
Nobby Ran off—from school. Approved school.

Shirley looks taken aback, but puts up a brave front

Shirley You must be round the twist.

Nobby turns to Rita and grabs her by the wrist

Nobby You did, didn't you?
Rita I don't know what you're on about, let go of me. (*She shakes herself free*)
Jeff Is that right, Nobby?
Nobby It's in the *Daily Mirror*. The police are after them.
Shirley Hear that, Reet? We're famous. We're in the papers.

In Need of Care

Rita What are we going to do, Shirl?
Shirley Nothing.

Shirley moves towards the door, but Nobby moves quicker and bars her way. Jeff and Rita watch, wondering what is going to happen. Nobby and Shirley eye each other defiantly, then Shirley's expression changes to a crafty grin

Nobody knows we are here, except you. You won't tell on us, will you, Nobby? I quite fancy you.

Shirley winks at Nobby and assumes what she believes to be a sexy pose. Nobby's resolve weakens as he finds her attractive, and he smirks at her

Shirley Well?
Nobby I don't know. What should we do, Jeff?
Jeff I don't know. I don't know what we should do.
Nobby We'll have to think about it. Come here, Jeff.

Jeff goes across to Nobby and they start to go out

Shirley Where are you going?
Nobby We'll be back.

Nobby and Jeff go out

Rita Let's pack it in, Shirl. I'm scared.
Shirley They won't tell.
Rita How do you know?
Shirley That Nobby. He fancies me like mad.
Rita Do you reckon so?
Shirley The way he looks at me. (*She begins to act like a screen vamp, posing in a sexy way and sitting on the upturned box, crossing her legs, pulling up her skirt to reveal as much of her thighs as possible*)
Rita That doesn't mean he won't tell.
Shirley He's a right randy one, I'm telling you.
Rita Shirl, what are you going to do?
Shirley Men are easy when you know how. (*She pulls her jumper over her head, smoothes down her blouse to show her figure to advantage*)

Rita looks very unhappy

Just tease 'em up a bit. I'll take Nobby, you take Jeff. Here.
(*She tosses her jumper to Rita*)
Rita No, Shirl, I don't want to.
Shirley You don't have to do nothing. Just make 'em think you will.
Rita Well, if you think it will work.
Shirley You leave it to me. All right?
Rita All right.
Shirley (*calling*) Nobby.
Nobby (*off*) What?
Shirley Come here.
Nobby (*putting his head round the door*) What for?
Shirley Come on.

Nobby and Jeff come in

Shirley What are you going to do?
Nobby We haven't decided yet.
Shirley Reet and I have been talking it over. We've decided to give ourselves up.
Nobby Oh yes?
Shirley But we don't want to go right away.
Jeff You might as well get it over with.
Shirley It's not that. But do you know what it's like at those schools? We never see no fellows. Leastways, not decent fellows like you two. So while we've got our freedom, like, well we want to make the best of it. Another hour won't make any difference, will it?
Nobby No, I don't suppose it will.

Shirley eyes Nobby provocatively

Shirley We could have a bit of fun, eh?
Jeff I don't know, Nobby.
Nobby Well, it couldn't do any harm.
Shirley Nobody will know you were here with us.
Nobby No, I suppose not.
Shirley Well?
Nobby Why not?
Shirley Well, come on then.

Shirley invites Nobby to sit beside her by means of her glance.

In Need of Care

Nobby sits beside her. Jeff and Rita stare at them

Nobby . . .
Nobby Yes?
Shirley I know we've only just met, but . . .

Shirley looks up and sees Rita staring at her

You're cramping my style, kid.

Rita goes to Jeff, takes his arm and leads him to one side

Rita You don't blame us, do you?
Jeff No, of course not. It must be pretty awful at those schools.
Shirley I know we've only just met you, but I quite fancy you.
Nobby (*looking down the front of Shirley's blouse*) You're not so bad yourself.
Shirley You got a girl?
Nobby No.
Shirley No kidding? A nice looking fellow like you?
Nobby Do you think so?
Shirley Sure. The girls round here must be blind or daft.
Nobby Oh, I don't know.
Shirley Perhaps you don't like girls?
Nobby Yes, I do. Well, some are all right.
Shirley Do you like me?
Nobby Yes. Yes, of course I do.

Shirley snuggles up close to Nobby, putting her face up to his

Shirley I know I'm not all that pretty, but I've got ever such a nice figure.
Nobby Yes. I mean about your figure.
Shirley It doesn't show so good in those awful clothes. You should see me in a bikini.
Nobby I bet you look real good.
Shirley Nobby.
Nobby Yes?

Shirley gently turns Nobby's face to hers. They kiss. Shirley breaks off the embrace, gets up and goes to the door. She looks out and then back at Nobby, inviting him with her eyes. Jeff watches Nobby disapprovingly. Rita sits with her head cupped in her hands, looking miserable

Shirley I think I'll go out for a breath of fresh air.
Nobby I think I'd better go with her, Jeff, in case she tries to run off.
Jeff (*sarcastically*) Oh, sure.

Nobby goes to Shirley. They put their arms round each other and go out

Jeff moves to the upturned box and sits down

I don't trust your friend.
Rita She's all right when you know her.

There is an awkward silence. Jeff whittles his stick. Rita eyes him cautiously

Jeff Did you sleep here last night?
Rita Yes.
Jeff Weren't you cold?
Rita Freezing.
Jeff It must have been pretty awful.
Rita It was.
Jeff Haven't you had anything to eat?
Rita No.
Jeff You must be hungry.
Rita Yes.
Jeff What shall we do?
Rita I don't know. What do you want to do?
Jeff I don't know.

Rita, after hesitation, suddenly moves over and stands quite close to Jeff

Rita You can kiss me if you want to.
Jeff Can I?
Rita Yes, if you want to.

Jeff is embarrassed

It's all right.
Jeff Well, later perhaps.

Rita looks relieved. She moves away and sits on a bale of straw

In Need of Care

Jeff What will they do to you?
Rita Who?
Jeff At the prison.
Rita It isn't a prison, it's a school.
Jeff Oh, yes. I'm sorry.
Rita It's all right.
Jeff Why did you run away?
Rita It was Shirley's idea.
Jeff Do you do everything she says?
Rita She's my mate. You don't half ask a lot of questions.
Jeff I didn't mean to be rude. But she doesn't seem to be a very good friend, if you don't mind my saying so.
Rita Why?
Jeff Well, you'll only get into more trouble.
Rita It's all right for you. What do you know about it?
Jeff I mean, the more you get into trouble, the longer you'll have to stay there, won't you?
Rita (*angrily*) I never asked to go there in the first place.

There is an awkward silence

Can't we talk about something else?
Jeff Like what?
Rita Well, anything. Is this really your dad's barn?
Jeff Yes, this is our farm.
Rita You own all this. This field and everything?
Jeff Yes, my dad's a farmer. There are lots of other fields too.
Rita You must be ever so rich.
Jeff No, I don't think we are.
Rita Do you like living on a farm?
Jeff I never thought about it. Yes, I suppose I do. We have lots of fun, but I have to do a lot of work too.
Rita Like?
Jeff Helping Dad.

Rita gets up and moves away

Rita I never had a dad.
Jeff I'm sorry.
Rita Leastways, not a real one.
Jeff What about your mum?
Rita I've got two mums. That's funny, isn't it, having two mums.

One's not my real one of course.
Jeff How do you mean?

Rita comes to Jeff and sits on a bale of straw near him

Rita (*telling her story with enthusiasm*) When I was little I was fostered. I thought they were my real mum and dad, I suppose. I never thought anything else. We lived in a lovely house and I had all nice things, like toys and clothes and things. We used to go out in Dad's car to the seaside and the zoo. (*Suddenly she stops and looks very sad*) Sometimes we used to—we used to . . .
Jeff Go on.

Rita bites her lip

Rita, you're crying.
Rita No, I'm not.
Jeff I didn't mean to pry.
Rita When I was about seven, Mum said I was to go and stay with an Aunt Cathie who I'd never seen before. I knew something was up because I saw Mum was crying. Then this Aunt Cathie came and took me away. I never saw Mummy again.
Jeff What about your real mother?
Rita Well, after a bit, Aunt Cathie tells me she's my real mum, and that the people I had lived with were just looking after me because she'd been ill, and hadn't got anywhere to live, and no money.
Jeff Didn't you like your real mother?
Rita She was kind at first, but after a bit she didn't seem to care any more. Then she used to shout at me, and hit me. Not all the time, but when she was in a bad mood.
Jeff Were there just the two of you?
Rita Sometimes. But she used to keep lodgers, leastways that's what she said they was. They was always men. They used to go out a lot at night. I was frightened on my own in the dark.
Jeff It must have been pretty awful for you.
Rita Sometimes there were terrible rows, and then she'd take it out on me. Like the time about the cat.
Jeff What happened?
Rita (*very bitterly*) It loved me. It wouldn't have run away from me. She killed it, I know she did.
Jeff I'm terribly sorry, Rita. We've got two dogs and a cat.

In Need of Care

Rita (*dully*) Have you?
Jeff One of the dogs, Bessie, is a black and white sheep dog. She's a working dog, out with Dad all day. Butch is just Mum's pet. I don't know what it is, a sort of mongrel, I suppose. The cat is ever so fluffy and smoky grey in colour. I think you would like him.
Rita I wish I could see them.
Jeff It's a bit difficult, isn't it? I mean, with you . . .
Rita Yes, I suppose it is.

There is an awkward silence. Rita looks very dejected and Jeff eyes her curiously

Jeff I've never met a girl like you before. How did you ever get sent to that place?
Rita One day there were some boys throwing stones at a dog. I tried to stop them. They were big boys, bigger than me. One of them got hold of me and was twisting my arm until I cried. I managed to get hold of a bit of wood and I hit him until he let go of me. Then he came at me again and I hit him as hard as I could on the head and knocked him out.
Jeff But he was . . .
Rita He was ever so ill for a long time. I don't know if he ever got better. I had to go to court.
Jeff And they sent you away for that?
Rita No, not that time. I was put on probation.
Jeff That's not fair. It wasn't your fault.
Rita Cathie didn't like Miss Western coming to the house, and she was always taking it out on me, saying that I was a criminal and no good, and what would the neighbours say, and all that. So in the end I ran away.
Jeff Where did you go?
Rita I didn't know what to do. I just wandered about all day, and then in the end I got into a posh house to try and find some food, and when I was in there I found some money and I took that instead. I went into a café to get something to eat, and when I was in there a copper came in and arrested me. The probation officer was ever so good in court, and said it wasn't my fault, and all about what it was like for me at home. The magistrate said that it wasn't supposed to be a punishment for what I'd done, but that I'd be better away from home, and that

the school would teach me to stop stealing things and hitting people on the head.
Jeff I'm ever so sorry, Rita. I don't think it was your fault. I wish I could help.

Jeff moves and sits beside Rita, who smiles at him

I could write to you at school.
Rita Would you?
Jeff Of course I would. And perhaps in the summer holidays you could come and stay on the farm.
Rita (*jumping up*) Oh, Jeff, could I?
Jeff I'd have to ask my mum and dad, of course.
Rita Jeff, you're not kidding me on, are you? I couldn't bear it if you were.
Jeff I can't promise you definitely, of course. But I'd try.
Rita Oh, Jeff, please.
Jeff What were you going to do before Nobby and I found you?
Rita We were going to Shirley's auntie's at first, and then I was going to go home.
Jeff But I thought you hated it at home?
Rita I mean to my foster-parents. That's my real home. They'd look after me, I know. And if I could live there, I wouldn't get into any more trouble, and they'd have to realize that and let me stay.

Jeff gets up and moves towards Rita

Jeff Rita.
Rita Yes?
Jeff I know this sounds daft, but . . .
Rita What, Jeff?
Jeff It doesn't matter.
Rita What is it, Jeff?
Jeff I don't suppose we shall ever see each other again.
Rita You said that I could come and stay at your farm. You said that.
Jeff I know, but people are so difficult. I mean . . .
Rita What's the good. We shall never see each other again.
Jeff We would if we waited long enough. They can't keep you there all your life.

In Need of Care 19

Rita You'd never wait.
Jeff Yes, I would. Honest I would.
Rita (*shyly*) I'm glad you didn't kiss me when I offered. I didn't want you to—then.
Jeff I know you didn't.
Rita I'm not like Shirley.
Jeff I know.

They look at each other. They want to kiss, but both are too shy to make the first move

   Rita.
Rita Yes.
Jeff You will go back to school? I mean you won't keep on running away?

Rita hesitates at first, and then smiles at Jeff

Rita Yes.
Jeff Promise?
Rita I promise.
Shirley (*off*) Do you mind if we come in?

Jeff and Rita move away from each other

Jeff Of course not.

   Shirley and Nobby come in arm in arm

Shirley Didn't want to interrupt anything, like.
Nobby Jeff, I promised Shirley we would get them some food before they go. Could you get some from your place?
Jeff Yes, I should think so.
Shirley Hurry up then. We're starving to death.

Nobby breaks away from Shirley

Nobby Come on then.
Shirley You won't split on us, will you?
Nobby 'Course not.

Jeff looks at Rita. Shirley watches them suspiciously

   Come on, Jeff.

Nobby and Jeff go out

Rita sits down on the straw. Shirley watches the boys from the door, then sits beside Rita

Shirley How did you get on, Reet?
Rita O.K.
Shirley Did he try anything?
Rita Not really.
Shirley You can't have got the right technique, kid.
Rita He's not like that.
Shirley Here, you don't reckon he'll split on us, do you?
Rita No, I don't reckon he will.
Shirley Nobby's all right. He won't dare tell.
Rita How do you know?
Shirley 'Cause I'd tell them about him.
Rita You didn't let him, did you, Shirl?
Shirley I couldn't half do with a fag.
Rita I couldn't do that.

Shirley gets up, picks up her pullover and puts it on

Shirley As soon as we've had some grub, we'll set off. Nobby showed me where to go. We are not far from the main road to London. There's lots of lorries on it, we can easy hitch a lift.

Shirley sits on the upturned box and watches carefully for Rita's reaction

Rita But we aren't going to London. You said we were going to your auntie's.
Shirley I've been thinking about it, Reet. It will be better to go to London.
Rita But I don't want to go to London.
Shirley It's no good going to my auntie's. We'll get caught.
Rita You never said that before.
Shirley I never thought about it before.
Rita I'm not going.
Shirley Why not?
Rita 'Cause I want to go home.
Shirley You must be off your nut. They'll only send you back.
Rita They won't. I know they won't.

In Need of Care

Shirley 'Course they will. Listen, kid, London is the place. They'll never find you there. There's plenty of work. Clubs and things. You can earn forty quid a week.
Rita Stop calling me kid. I'm not going.

Shirley becomes angry and frustrated. She picks up a piece of wood and throws it across the barn in a flash of temper.

Shirley Well, you go back to that stinking old school if you want to. And when you get fed up with all them old bags ordering you about, you just think of me. You do just that. You think of me earning forty quid a week, all dressed up in posh clothes, living in a lovely flat, having parties with all them smashing fellows.
Rita I can't help it.
Shirley You don't want to go back, do you?
Rita No, of course I don't.
Shirley You must be mad.
Rita I want to go home.
Shirley We've always been good mates, haven't we?
Rita Yes, Shirl.
Shirley I've never let you down, have I?
Rita No.
Shirley Then listen, kid. If you come to London with me, once we get settled and clear of the law, you can go home any time you like.
Rita I don't know, Shirl. I promised.
Shirley Promised? Who?
Rita Jeff
Shirley What?
Rita I'd give myself up.
Shirley You silly great nit. What did you want to go and do that for.
Rita He's nice.
Shirley You stuck on him?
Rita He's ever so nice and kind.
Shirley What good is that going to do you when you're back in that school?
Rita He said he'd write to me.
Shirley And you believed that?
Rita Yes.

Shirley You're dafter than I thought you were. Don't you know about men yet?
Rita They're not all bad.
Shirley They're all after one thing.
Rita Jeff's not like that. He never tried to touch me, and I offered. Honestly, Shirl, he's different. He's a real smashing bloke.
Shirley You're really stuck on him, aren't you?
Rita I think he likes me.
Shirley Did he say that?
Rita Sort of.
Shirley Well, you don't want to trust him.
Rita I don't know what to believe.
Shirley I shouldn't think you do. Listen, kid, I don't really care what happens to you. (*Very angry*) You can go to hell if you want to. But don't you bloody well get in my way and stop me getting to London.
Rita Don't, Shirl. Don't shout at me. You're my friend.
Shirley A good friend you are, letting me down like this. I suppose once they get their hands on you, you'll tell them everything about me going to London and everything.
Rita I won't, Shirl. I promise I won't. I wouldn't grass on you.
Shirley Oh, what the hell. I wish those blokes would come back with that food.

Shirley lies down on the straw. After a second Rita sits down beside her

Rita Shirl.
Shirley What?
Rita I'm sorry. I don't want to let you down. I don't know what to do. I'm so tired and hungry. At least there's food at that place, and some of the screws aren't all that bad. When I leave school I could go back to my mum and dad, and perhaps some day some nice bloke like Jeff will marry me, and everything will be all right.
Shirley Stop dreaming, kid. They'll never let you. They took you away from your mum and dad, didn't they?
Rita Did I ever tell you about what it was like then?

Shirley Hundreds of times.
Rita We used to have a cat called Blackie. He had lovely green eyes and a wisp of white down his front. He used to sleep on my bed, and I'd stroke him and stroke him, and he'd purr louder and louder until I fell asleep. We had a nice garden, all flowers and things. In the summer we used to put up a tent, and my friend would come in, and we'd play nurses and patients. We'd bandage up all our dolls and make them better. There used to be a river. Mummy gave us fishing nets and we used to paddle and catch minnows and put them in a jam jar. At first I took them home, but they used to die, so after that I just used to look at them for a bit, and then put them back. (*She starts to cry*) I don't think I want to go on, unless I can have happy times like that again. I think I'd rather die.

Rita breaks down completely and sobs uncontrollably. Shirley is moved and sits up and comforts her

Shirley Don't say that, Reet. Don't ever say things like that, love. If only you wasn't so soft. You can't stand up against them. All them coppers and screws and magistrates and all that lot. If you want to go back, you go back. Don't you worry about me.
Rita If only I was tough like you.
Shirley You can't help it. I was just made different, that's all.
Rita They're not all bad, are they? Not all of them?
Shirley No, I suppose not. It's just that I never met the good ones. Perhaps your Jeff is good, perhaps he will marry you. Perhaps everything will turn out good for you. Come on, kid, dry your eyes. (*She hands Rita her handkerchief*)
Rita Thanks, Shirl. I'm sorry I bawled.

Nobby and Jeff come in. Jeff has a carrier bag of food. They put the bag on the upturned box and take out two apples, a bottle of milk, a piece of cake and some biscuits

Nobby We thought you might have gone.

Shirley comes over, sorts out the food and starts to eat

Shirley Coo, that's smashing. Come on, Reet, grub.

Rita comes over

Jeff It's the best we could do.
Shirley Here you are, Reet.

The girls eat the food greedily

Nobby We thought we ought to warn you.
Shirley *(alert)* What?
Nobby Coppers. The place is full of them. They know you are somewhere around here.
Shirley You didn't tell, did you?
Nobby We didn't tell anyone.

Shirley goes to the window and looks out

Shirley They're getting too ruddy close for my liking. Here, give us a drink of that milk.

Shirley grabs the bottle of milk from Rita and drinks. Rita turns and catches Jeff's eye. She averts her gaze

Jeff Rita

Rita looks at Shirley, then at the floor

Rita, come here.

Rita looks at Jeff and goes to him

What are you going to do?
Rita You did mean what you said, about writing.

Jeff pulls out a notebook and pencil

Jeff Here, your name and address.

Rita hesitates, then takes the notebook and pencil and starts to write. They smile at each other. Shirley comes from the window, watches Rita for a moment, takes up the handbag, puts an apple into it, takes out the handkerchief with the money in it, looks at it and then tosses it to Rita

Shirley Here, kid. I'm off.

Shirley goes to the door, looks out, and then comes back to Jeff

Listen, you. You'd better be on the level with Reet. She's been

In Need of Care

hurt too much. (*She turns to Rita*) So long, Reet. Good luck, kid.
Rita Shirl, I didn't mean to . . .
Shirley Forget it. So long, Nobby. Don't do nothing I wouldn't do.
Nobby So long.

Shirley goes out through the door

Nobby follows her to the door and watches her go

I doubt if she'll make it.

Rita and Jeff stand looking at each other. Jeff puts out his hand and Rita takes it

Rita I'm frightened, Jeff.
Jeff Do you want me to come with you?
Rita No. Don't get involved.
Nobby The coppers.
Rita Jeff.
Jeff It will be all right.
Nobby They're going down towards the path.

Rita goes to the door

Rita Is that the way Shirley went?
Nobby Yes. They'll see her in a minute.
Rita I'm going.
Jeff Just a minute, Reet.
Rita No. I must divert them from Shirley. Good-bye, Jeff.

Jeff goes to her at the door

Jeff Good luck.
Rita Please write.
Jeff I promise.

Jeff and Rita kiss very quickly, then Rita exits

The boys watch for a moment

They've seen her.

Nobby And Shirley, too. Just look at that copper running. Just as well, couple of tramps.
Jeff Leave her alone, you great big-headed copper. Holding her like that. She's only a kid.
Nobby You're real gone on that girl, aren't you, Jeff?
Jeff She's all right.
Nobby You don't want to get mixed up with the likes of her.
Jeff She's had a bad break.

Nobby goes and rummages in the tea chest

Nobby She's no good or she wouldn't be in the nick.
Jeff You never saw her when she was telling me.
Nobby O.K., mate, have it your own way.
Jeff Here, she never gave me back my pencil and notebook.
Nobby What did I tell you? She'd nick her grandmother's false teeth.
Jeff You're wrong, Nobby, she just forgot in the excitement.
Nobby Sure she did.

Jeff moves back into the barn. He sees the notebook lying on the floor, picks it up, and looks at the page where she has written her address. Nobby watches him

You're nuts.

CURTAIN

PRODUCTION NOTES

Boxes or rostra built up into a pyramid shape and covered with a neutral coloured backcloth and loose straw will give a very realistic effect of a pile of loose straw. The use of mattresses or pillows will help to break up the square angles of the boxes to give a more irregular shape. Hay can be used as an alternative to straw and looks just as effective.

The girls, when lying down should be at least 2 feet above the stage floor level, preferably each at different levels.

The set should be cluttered up with as much junk as possible without impeding the movement of the actors, and should produce an effect of neglect, dust and cobwebs.

The girls can be dressed in any sort of school uniform, but all of the characters should have some bright contrasting colour about their clothes to counteract the drabness of the set which will be predominated by greys, browns and yellows.

On the opening curtain, the sound of dogs barking in the distance will help to create the atmosphere of the countryside.

FURNITURE AND PROPERTY LIST

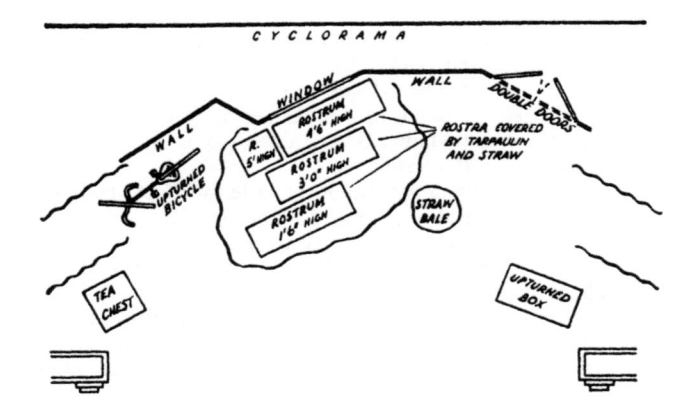

On stage: A number of rostra or boxes built up into a pyramid and covered by tarpaulin, straw, bits of sacking
Rusty bicycle
Tea chest. *In it:* motor-cycle carburettor, small pieces of machinery
Upturned box
Straw bales and loose straw

On walls: horse harness, hose pipe, farm implements, tools of all kinds

On shelves: used paint pots, old bottles, etc.

On floor: dead mouse; handkerchief tied in knots and containing coins; handbag containing crisp bag with 2 crisps, mirror, comb, lipstick

Off stage: Stick (**Jeff**)
Jack-knife (**Jeff**)

In Need of Care 29

Carrier with 2 apples, bottle of milk, pieces of cake.
biscuits (**Nobby**)
Notebook and pencil (**Jeff**)

Personal: **Shirley**: handkerchief

LIGHTING PLOT

Property fittings required: nil
Interior: a farm building
THE APPARENT SOURCES OF LIGHT are a door up L and window C, other windows in the "fourth wall"

To open: Morning
Fairly dim overall lighting, with spots on main acting areas, pile of straw, and upturned box. Strong daylight on backing

No cues

EFFECTS PLOT

Cue 1 On CURTAIN up (Page 1)
Distant barking of dogs. Continue until dialogue established

Lightning Source UK Ltd.
Milton Keynes UK
UKHW022002110319
338907UK00011BA/355/P